Lorne Michaels   Stuart Thompson   Sonia Friedman

Paramount Pictures   Marisa Sechrest   Ars Nova Entertainment   Berlind Productions
Steve Burke   Scott M. Delman   Roy Furman   Robert Greenblatt   Ruth Hendel   Jam Theatricals   The John Gore Organization
The Lowy Salpeter Company   James L. Nederlander   Christine Schwarzman   Universal Theatrical Group
Executive Producer David Turner

present

T0082033

Book by	Music by	Lyrics by
Tina Fey	**Jeff Richmond**	**Nell Benjamin**

Based on the Paramount Pictures film *Mean Girls*

with

Erika Henningsen   Taylor Louderman

Ashley Park   Kate Rockwell

Barrett Wilbert Weed   Grey Henson

Kerry Butler   Kyle Selig   Cheech Manohar   Rick Younger

Stephanie Lynn Bissonnette Tee Boyich Collins Conley Ben Cook DeMarius R. Copes Kevin Csolak Devon Hadsell
Curtis Holland Myles McHale Chris Medlin Brittany Nicholas Becca Petersen Nikhil Saboo
Jonalyn Saxer Brendon Stimson Riza Takahashi Kamille Upshaw Zurin Villanueva Gianna Yanelli Iain Young

Scenic Design	Costume Design	Lighting Design	Sound Design	Video Design
Scott Pask	**Gregg Barnes**	**Kenneth Posner**	**Brian Ronan**	**Finn Ross & Adam Young**

Hair Design	Makeup Design	Casting	Production Stage Manager
Josh Marquette	**Milagros Medina-Cerdeira**	**Telsey + Company** **Bethany Knox, CSA**	**Holly Coombs**

Orchestrations	Dance & Incidental Music Arrangements	Vocal Arrangements	Music Coordinator
John Clancy	**Glen Kelly**	**Mary-Mitchell Campbell Jeff Richmond** **Natalie Tenenbaum**	**Howard Joines**

Associate Director	Associate Choreographer	Production Management	Associate Producers
Casey Hushion	**John MacInnis**	**Aurora Productions**	**Micah Frank** **Caroline Maroney**

Press Representative	Advertising & Marketing	Digital Marketing	General Management
Boneau/Bryan-Brown	**SpotCo**	**Situation Interactive**	**Thompson Turner Productions** **Rebecca Habel & Adam J. Miller**

Music Direction
Mary-Mitchell Campbell

Directed and Choreographed by
Casey Nicholaw

ISBN 978-1-5400-8188-9

For all works contained herein:
Unauthorized copying, arranging, adapting, recording, Internet posting, public performance,
or other distribution of the music in this publication is an infringement of copyright.
Infringers are liable under the law.

Visit Hal Leonard Online at
www.halleonard.com

Contact us:
Hal Leonard
7777 West Bluemound Road
Milwaukee, WI 53213
Email: info@halleonard.com

In Europe, contact:
Hal Leonard Europe Limited
42 Wigmore Street
Marylebone, London, W1U 2RN
Email: info@halleonardeurope.com

In Australia, contact:
Hal Leonard Australia Pty. Ltd.
4 Lentara Court
Cheltenham, Victoria, 3192 Australia
Email: info@halleonard.com.au

3   **APEX PREDATOR**

8   **I SEE STARS**

15   **I'D RATHER BE ME**

24   **REVENGE PARTY**

36   **SEXY**

31   **SOMEONE GETS HURT**

42   **STUPID WITH LOVE**

56   **WHAT'S WRONG WITH ME?**

49   **WHERE DO YOU BELONG?**

60   **WORLD BURN**

APEX PREDATOR

Words by NELL BENJAMIN
Music by JEFF RICHMOND

Copyright © 2018 Useful Yak Music and Jeffrey Richmond Music
All Rights Administered Worldwide by Kobalt Songs Music Publishing
All Rights Reserved   Used by Permission

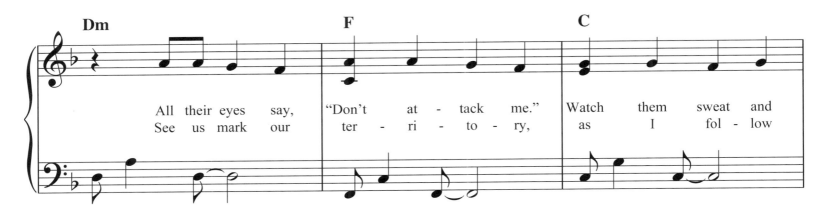

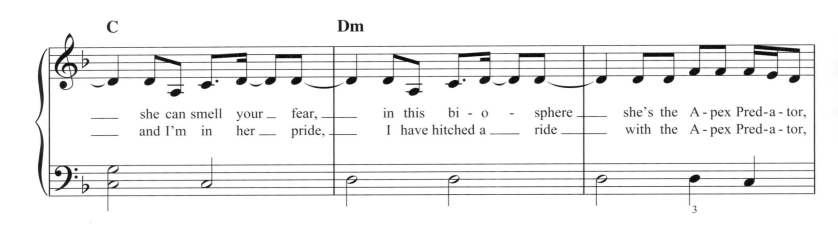

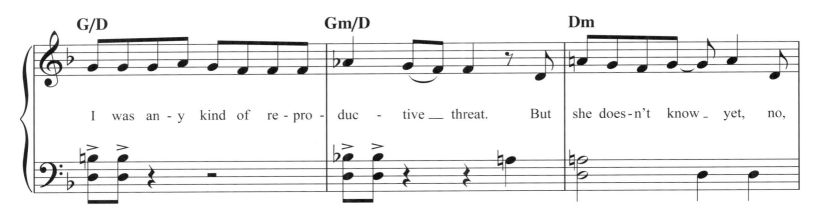

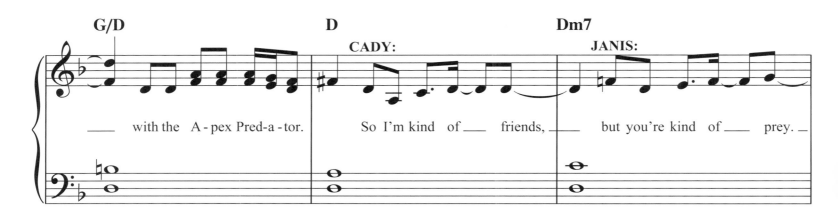

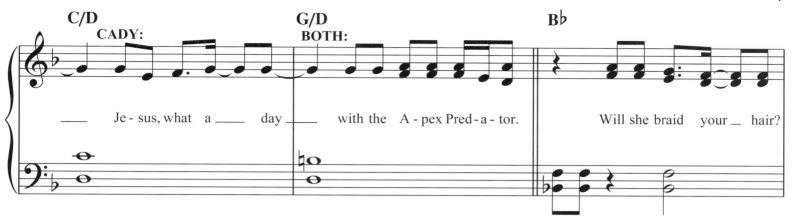

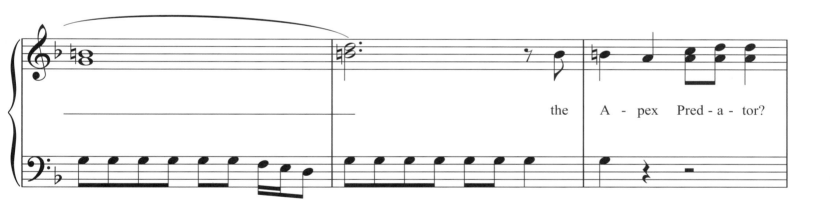

I SEE STARS

Words by NELL BENJAMIN
Music by JEFF RICHMOND

Copyright © 2018 Useful Yak Music and Jeffrey Richmond Music
All Rights Administered Worldwide by Kobalt Songs Music Publishing
All Rights Reserved   Used by Permission

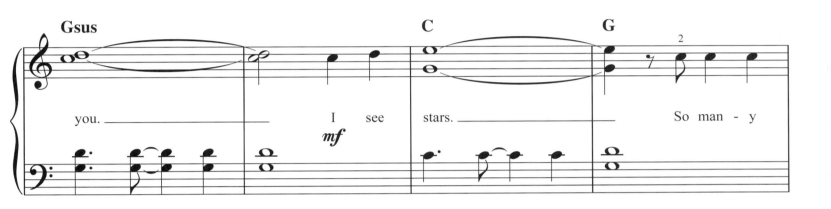

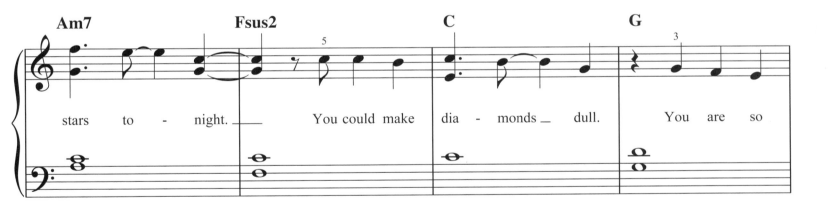

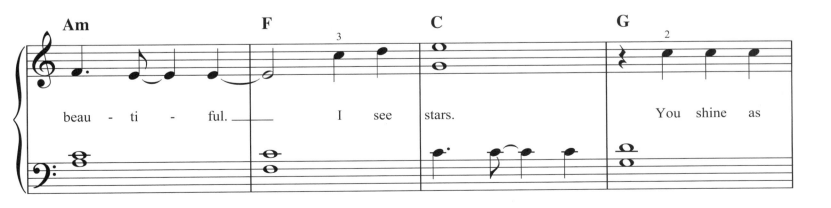

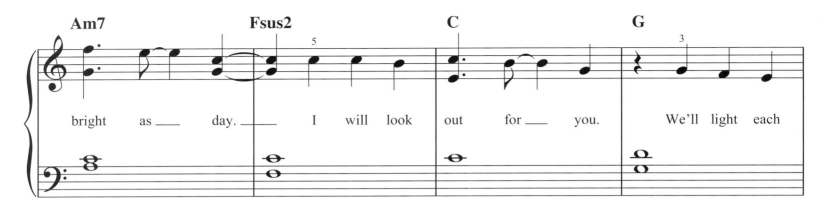

dark - er the night _ the bright - er you shine. Plas - tic don't shine, _

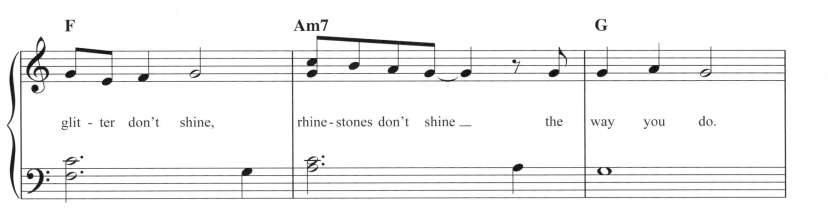

glit - ter don't shine, rhine - stones don't shine _ the way you do.

You are on fire. You can rise high'r. Up in the sky, en - joy the

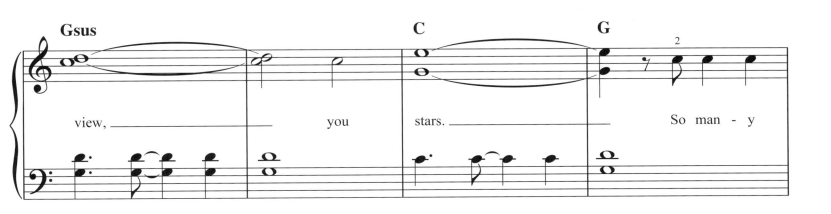

view, _ you stars. _ So man - y

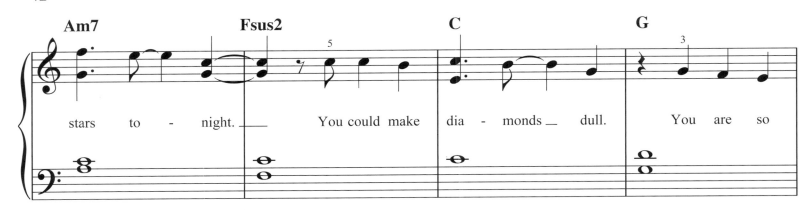

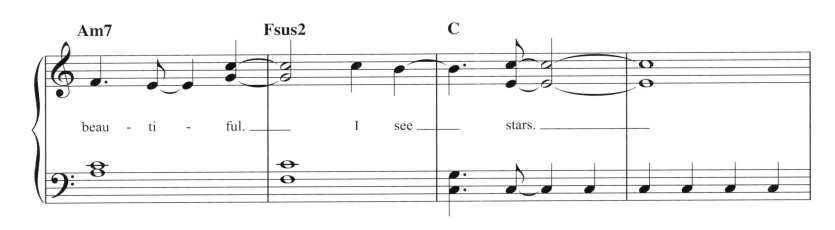

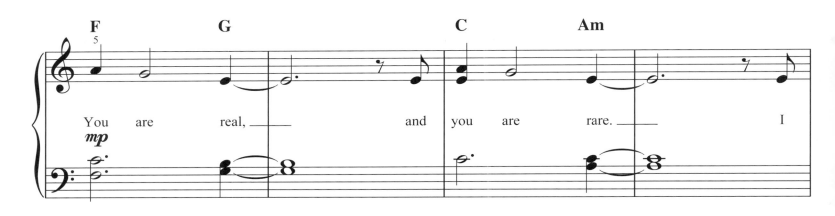

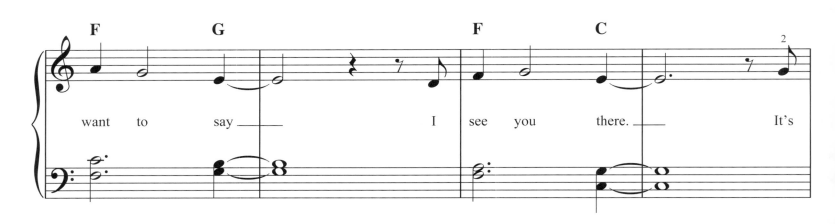

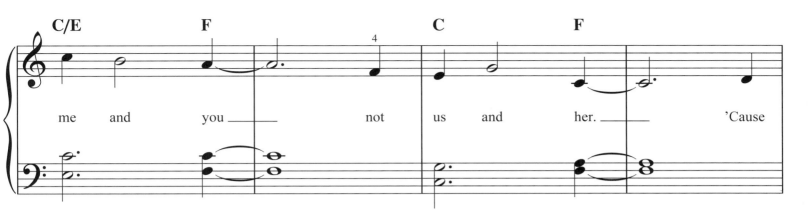

me and you ___ not us and her. ___ 'Cause

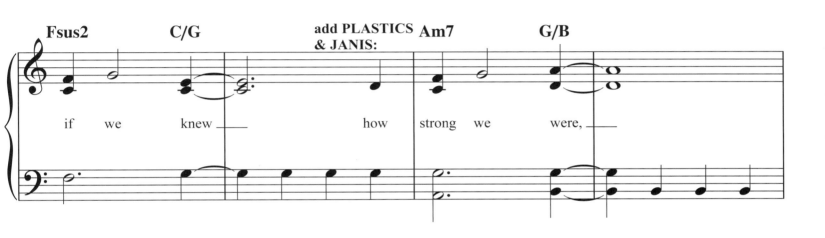

if we knew ___ how strong we were, ___

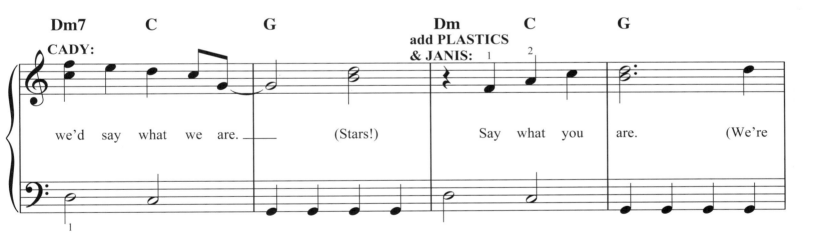

we'd say what we are. ___ (Stars!) Say what you are. (We're

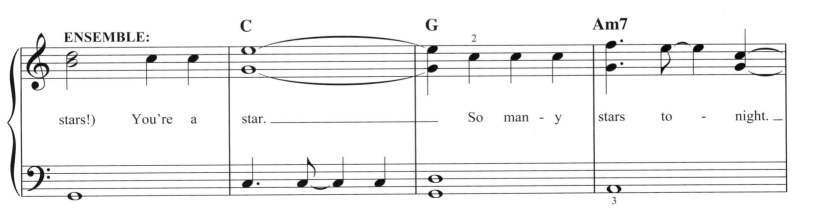

stars!) You're a star. ___ So man-y stars to-night. ___

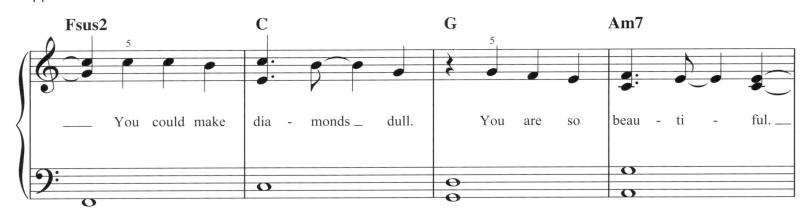

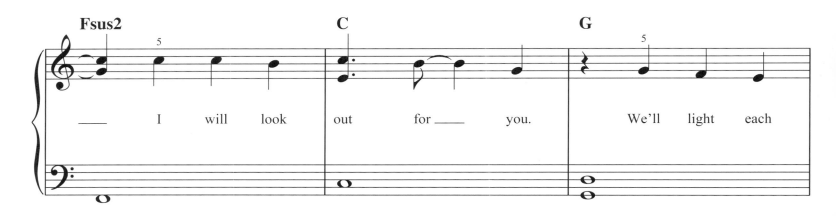

I'D RATHER BE ME

Words by NELL BENJAMIN
Music by JEFF RICHMOND

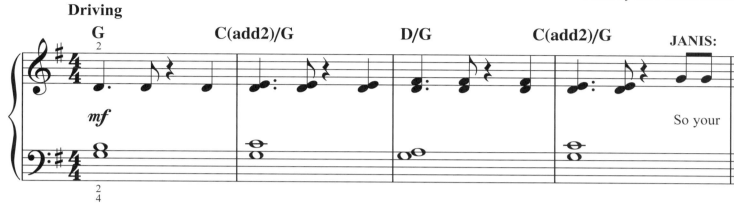

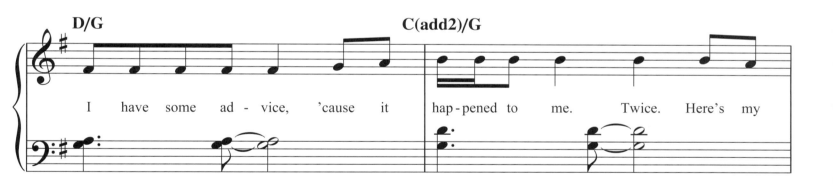

Copyright © 2018 Useful Yak Music and Jeffrey Richmond Music
All Rights Administered Worldwide by Kobalt Songs Music Publishing
All Rights Reserved   Used by Permission

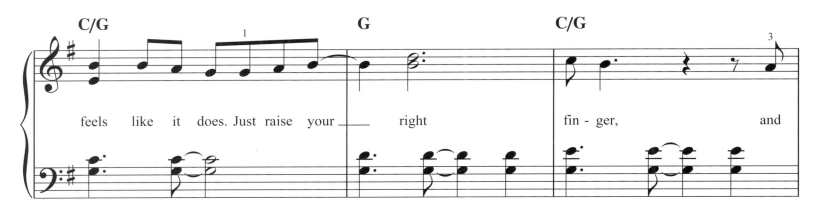

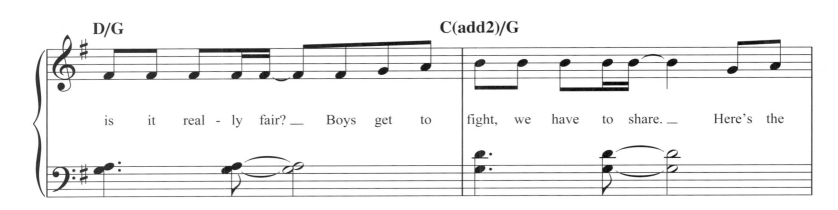

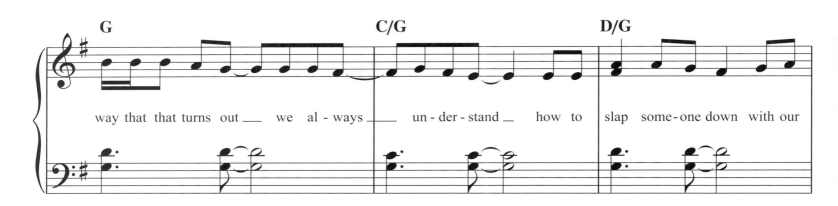

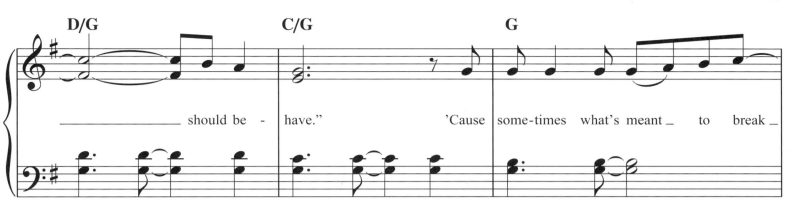

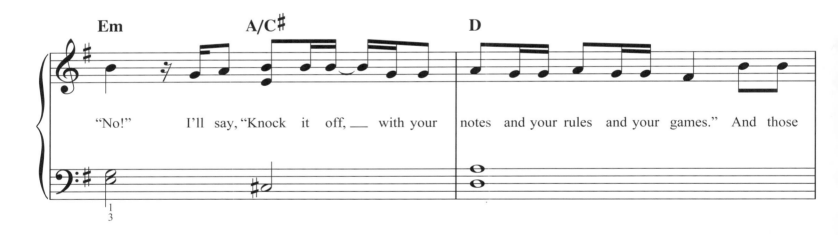

drag you down like they in - ev - i - ta - bly do, I will not laugh a - long with them and ap-

prove their pal - ace coup, 'cause that's not me. I don't

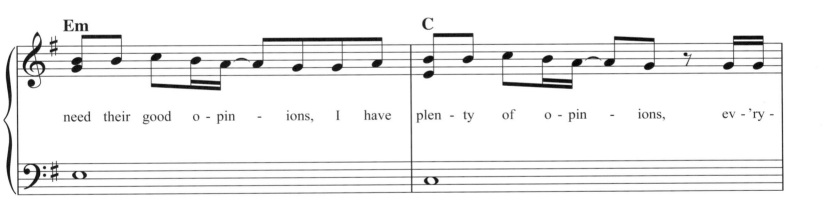

need their good o - pin - ions, I have plen - ty of o - pin - ions, ev - 'ry-

bod - y has o - pin - ions, but it does-n't make them true. __ What's true is be - ing me. __ I'd

rath - er be me, I'd rath - er be me than be with

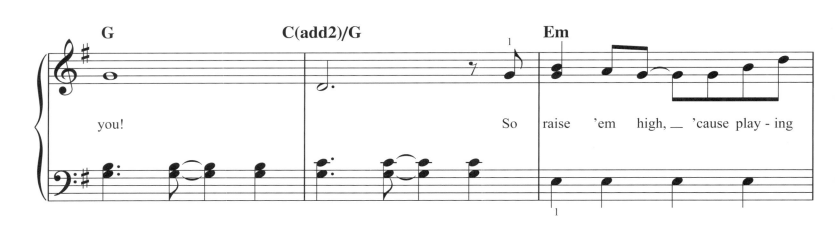

you! So raise 'em high, __ 'cause play - ing

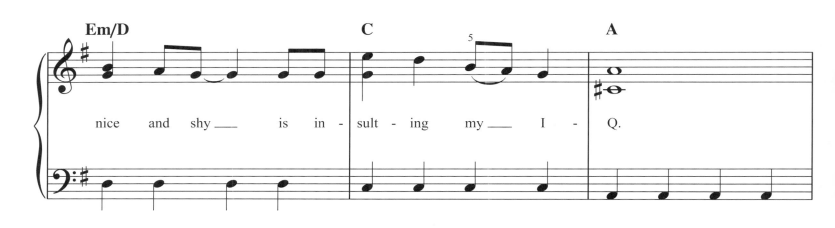

nice and shy __ is in - sult - ing my __ I - Q.

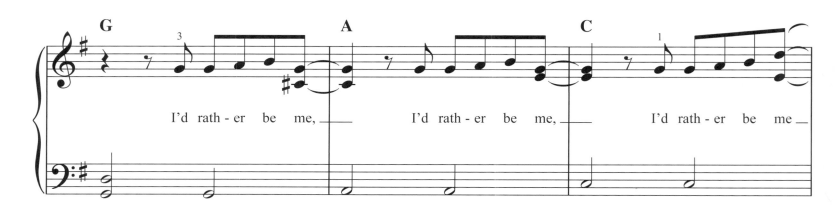

I'd rath - er be me, __ I'd rath - er be me, __ I'd rath - er be me __

than be with you! I'd rath-er be me, I'd rath-er be

me, I'd rath-er be me than be

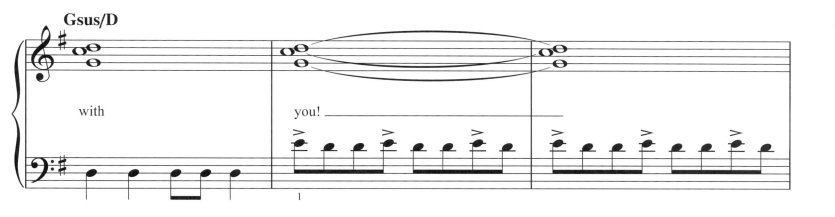

with you!

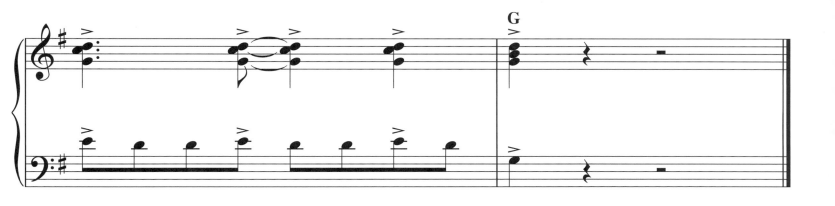

REVENGE PARTY

Words by NELL BENJAMIN
Music by JEFF RICHMOND

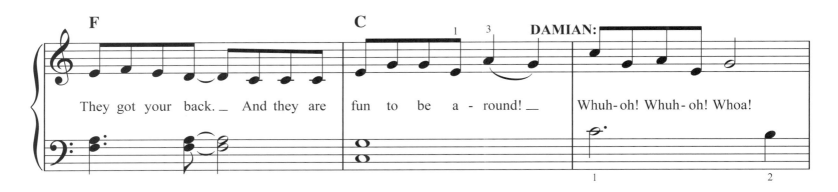

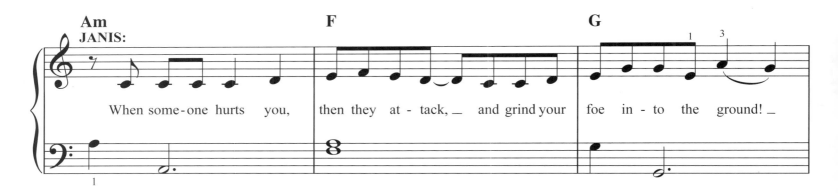

Copyright © 2018 Useful Yak Music and Jeffrey Richmond Music
All Rights Administered Worldwide by Kobalt Songs Music Publishing
All Rights Reserved   Used by Permission

C **F** **Dm**

sing-ing and danc - ing and cake! ___ And there's a mag - ic act ___ that saws Re-

C/E **F** **G**

gi - na in half, and this time it - 'll take! ___

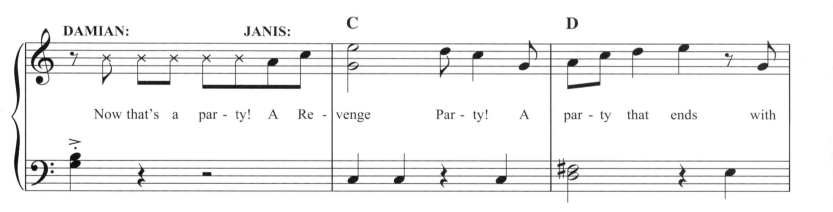

DAMIAN: **JANIS:** **C** **D**

Now that's a par - ty! A Re - venge Par - ty! A par - ty that ends with

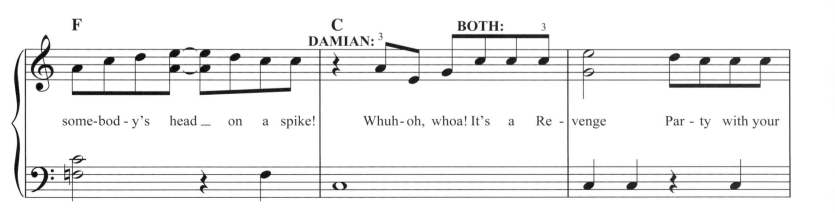

F **C** **BOTH:**

DAMIAN:

some-bod - y's head ___ on a spike! Whuh-oh, whoa! It's a Re - venge Par - ty with your

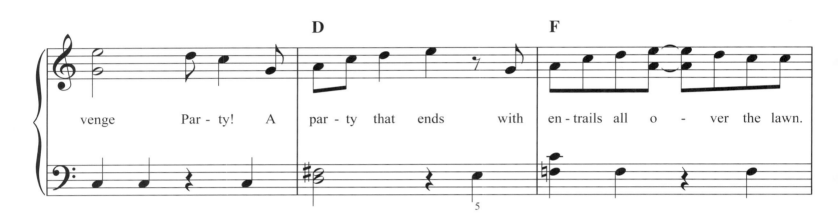

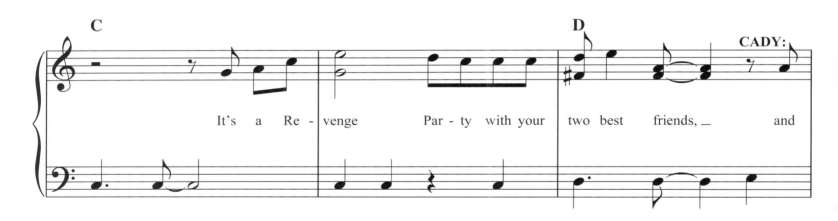

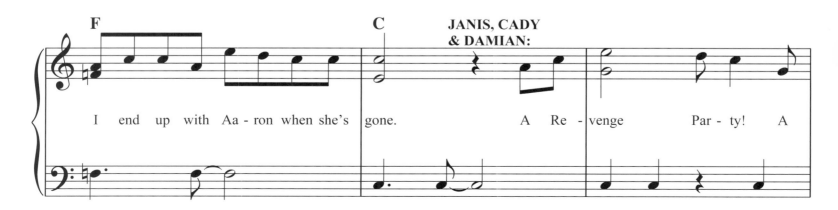

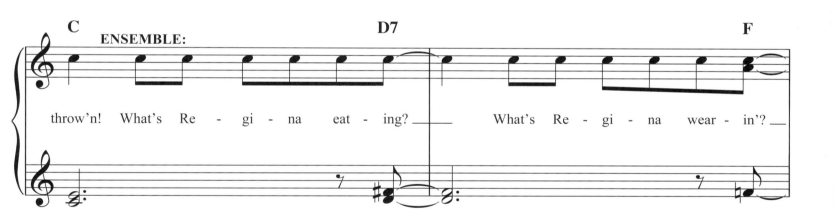

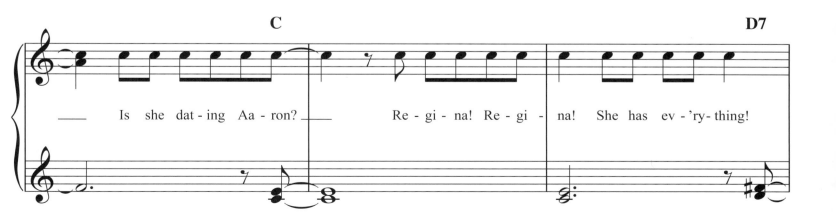

She gets ev-'ry-thing!

Re - gi - na! Re - gi - na! Re - gi - na!

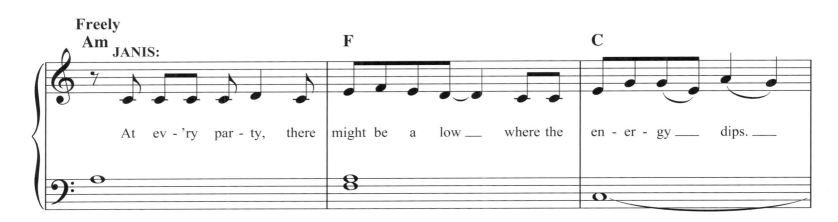

Freely

JANIS: At ev-'ry par-ty, there might be a low___ where the en-er-gy___ dips.___

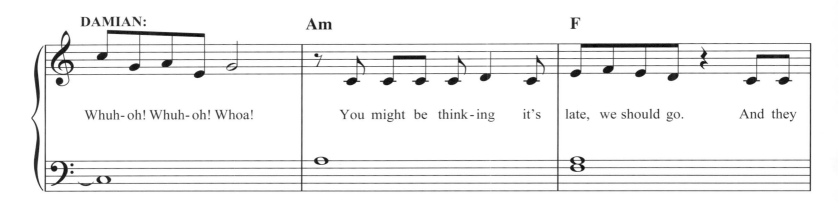

DAMIAN: Whuh-oh! Whuh-oh! Whoa! You might be think-ing it's late, we should go. And they

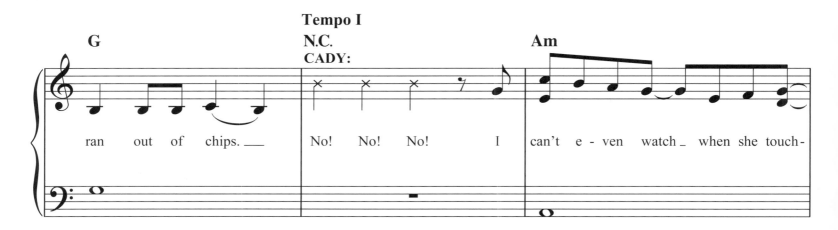

ran out of chips.___

Tempo I

N.C.
CADY: No! No! No! I can't e-ven watch___ when she touch-

- es his hair, and I watched a snake __ eat a cow! Re - gi - na

needs to be top-pled, sor - ry, Gret-chen, I swear. We'll get our par - ty now! __

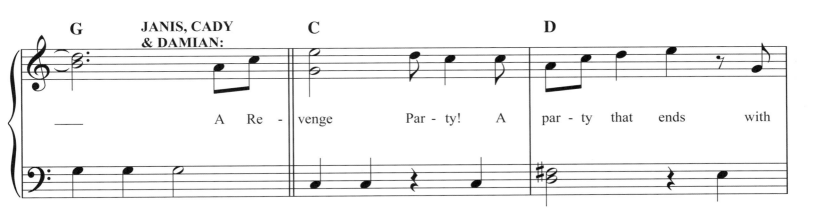

__ A Re - venge Par - ty! A par - ty that ends with

JANIS, CADY & DAMIAN:

li - ons in a Ro-man a - re - na! A Re - venge Par - ty with your

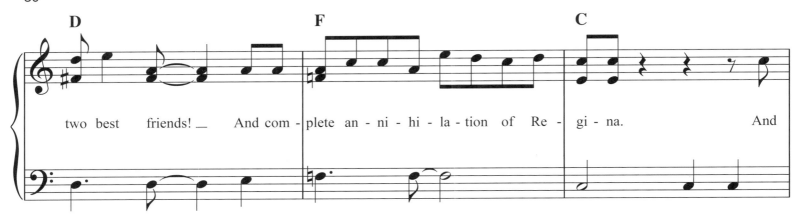

two best friends! __ And com-plete an-ni-hi-la-tion of Re-gi-na. And

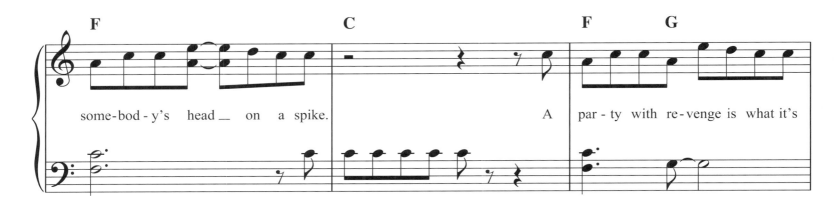

some-bod-y's head __ on a spike. A par-ty with re-venge is what it's

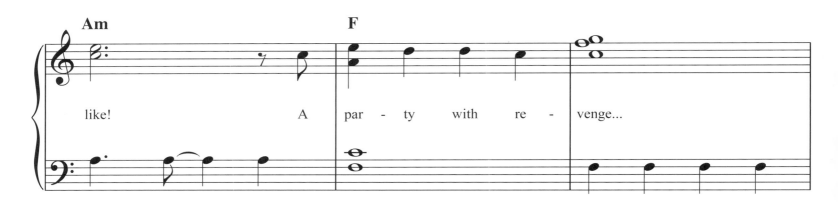

like! A par-ty with re-venge...

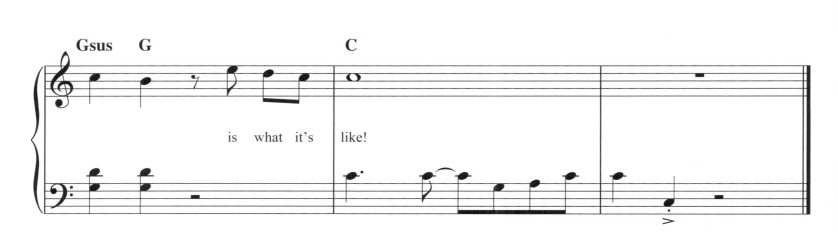

is what it's like!

SOMEONE GETS HURT

Words by NELL BENJAMIN
Music by JEFF RICHMOND

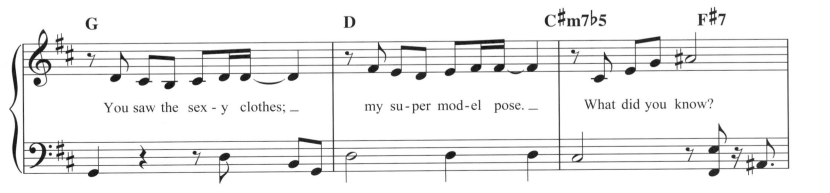

Copyright © 2018 Useful Yak Music and Jeffrey Richmond Music
All Rights Administered Worldwide by Kobalt Songs Music Publishing
All Rights Reserved Used by Permission

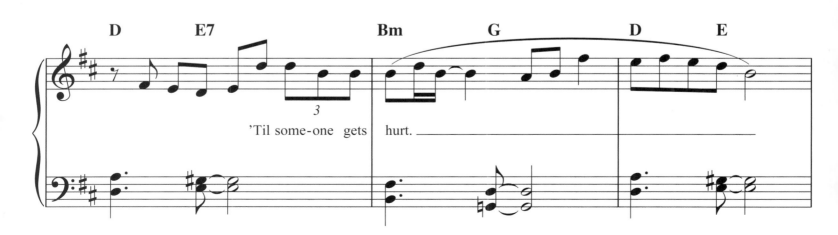

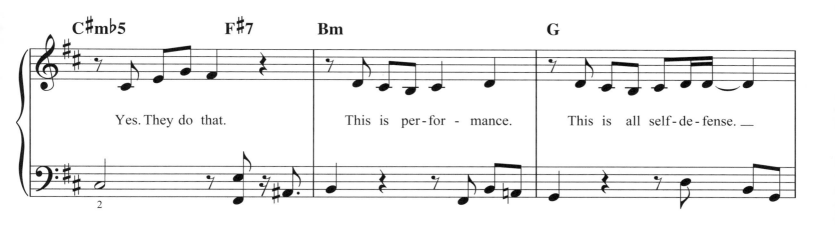

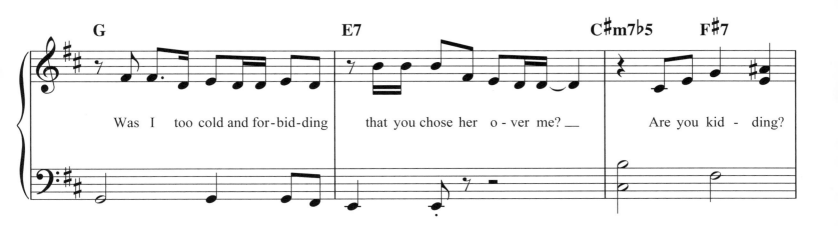

Poor lit - tle me, all trapped in this fab - u - lous

show! You could set me free, but if you're go - ing,

go! It's fine for you. It's fine to flirt and

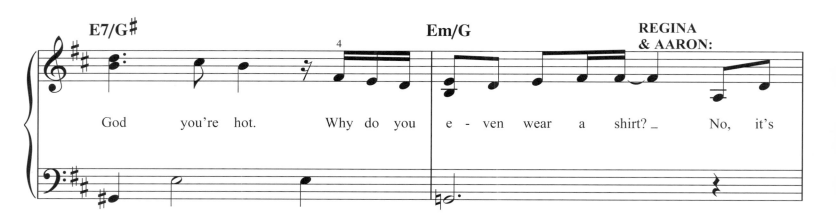

REGINA & AARON:

God you're hot. Why do you e - ven wear a shirt? ___ No, it's

fine. _____ Damn you're fine _____ and it's fine _____

WOMEN:
_____ 'til some-one gets... Ah! _____

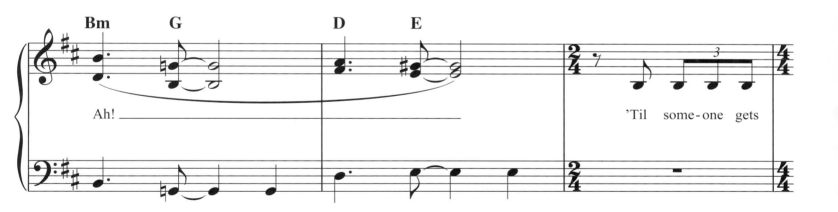

Ah! _____ 'Til some-one gets

hurt. 'Til some-one gets hurt.

SEXY

Words by NELL BENJAMIN
Music by JEFF RICHMOND

Copyright © 2018 Useful Yak Music and Jeffrey Richmond Music
All Rights Administered Worldwide by Kobalt Songs Music Publishing
All Rights Reserved   Used by Permission

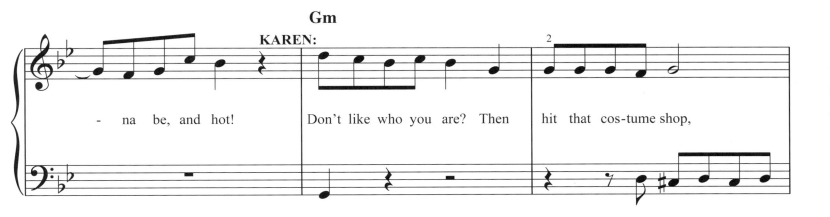

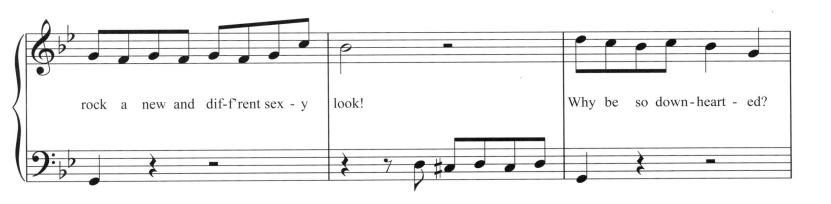

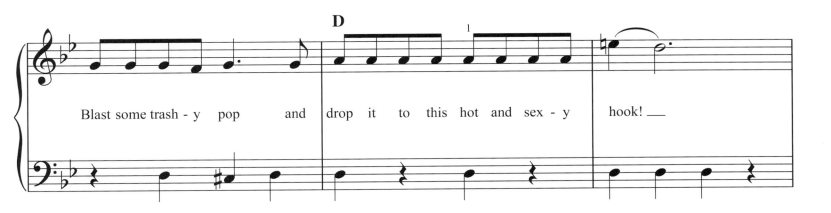

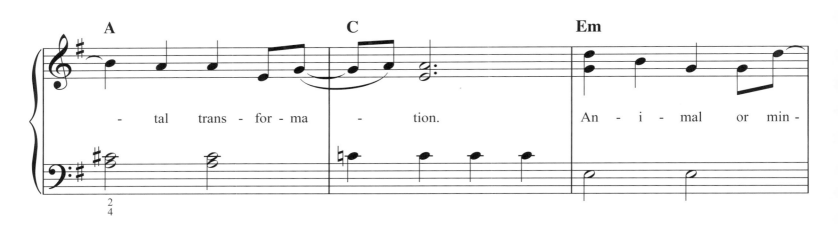

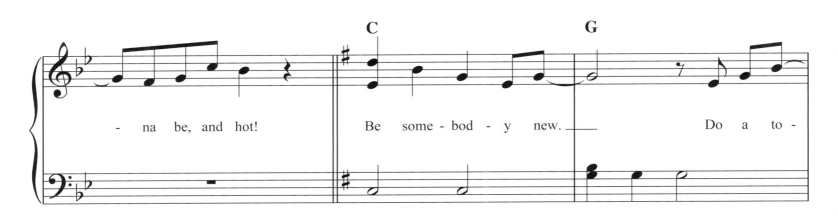

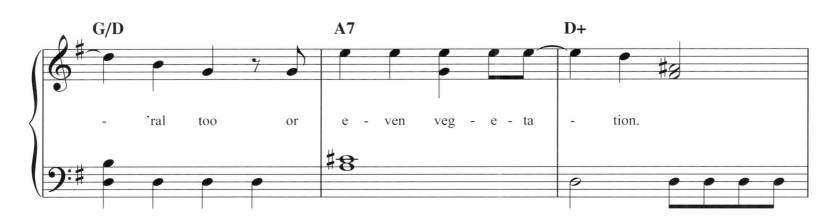

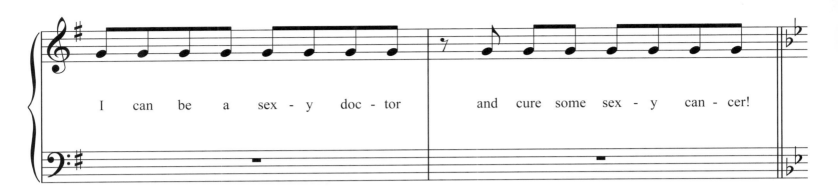

I can be a sex-y doc-tor and cure some sex-y can-cer!

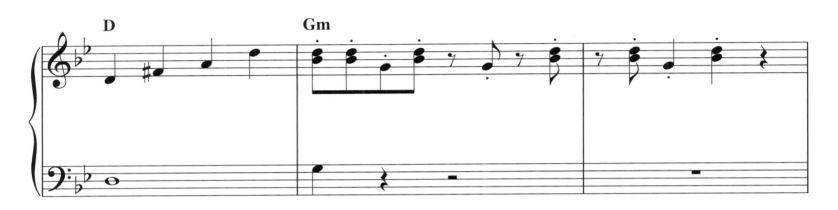

KAREN & WOMEN:

Hap-py Hal-low-een!

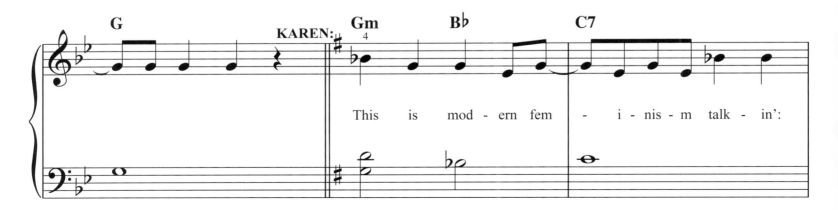

KAREN:

This is mod-ern fem - i-nis-m talk-in':

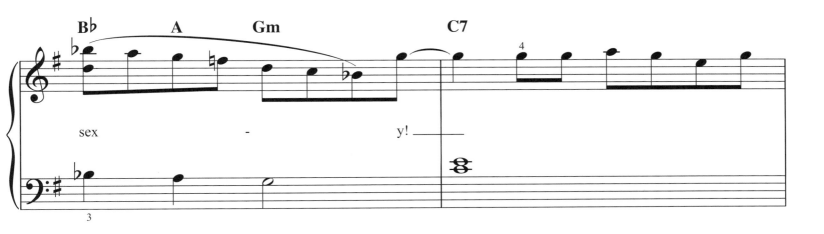

STUPID WITH LOVE

Words by NELL BENJAMIN
Music by JEFF RICHMOND

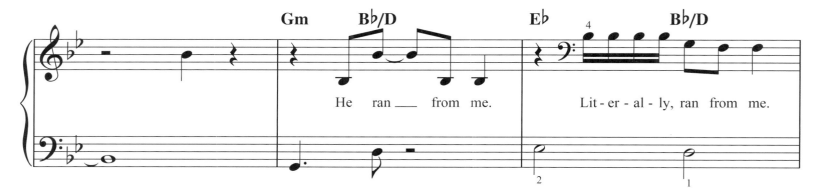

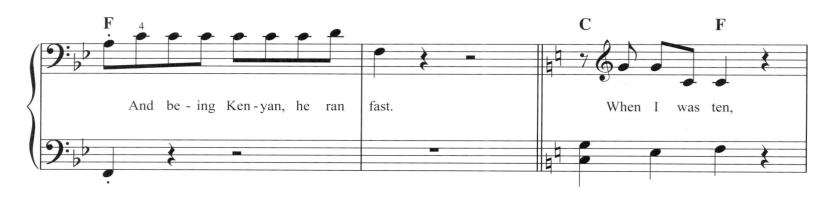

Copyright © 2018 Useful Yak Music and Jeffrey Richmond Music
All Rights Administered Worldwide by Kobalt Songs Music Publishing
All Rights Reserved   Used by Permission

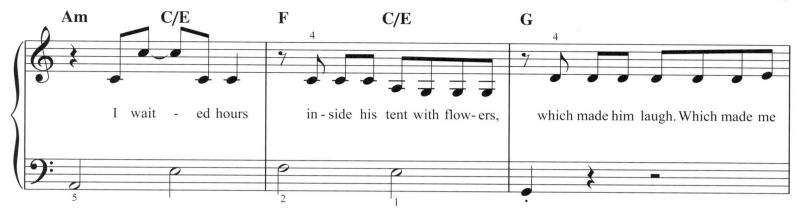

I wait - ed hours in - side his tent with flow - ers, which made him laugh. Which made me

African feel, bright tempo

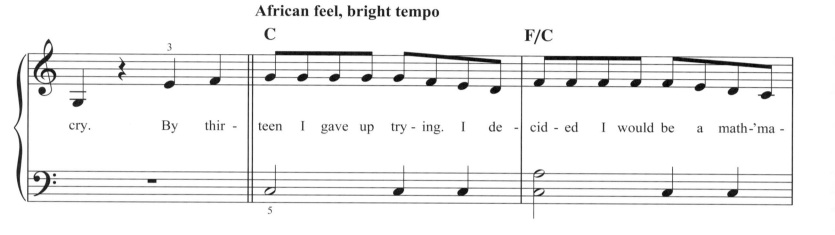

cry. By thir - teen I gave up try - ing. I de - cid - ed I would be a math-'ma -

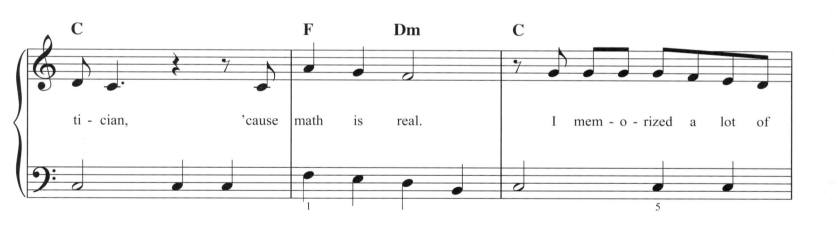

ti - cian, 'cause math is real. I mem - o - rized a lot of

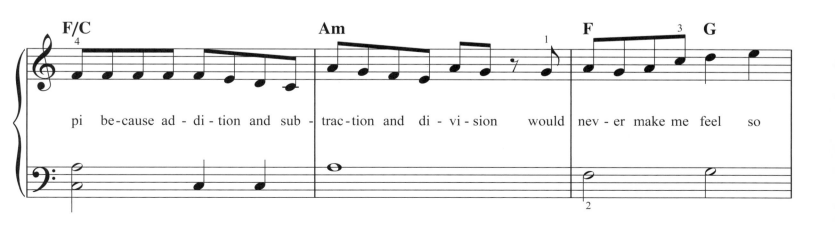

pi be-cause ad - di - tion and sub - trac-tion and di - vi - sion would nev - er make me feel so

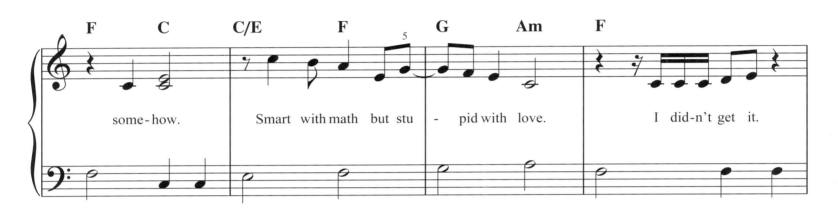

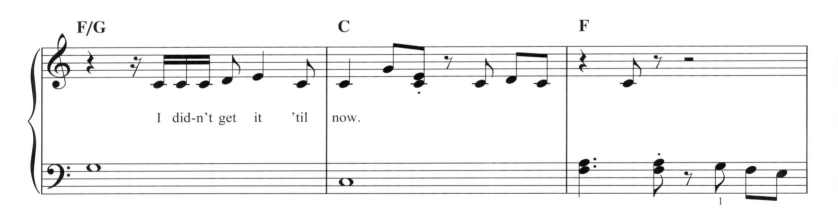

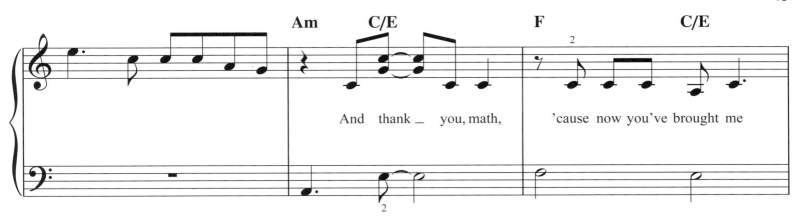

And thank _ you, math, 'cause now you've brought me

this cute boy! He's like some-one from T - V. He's like that

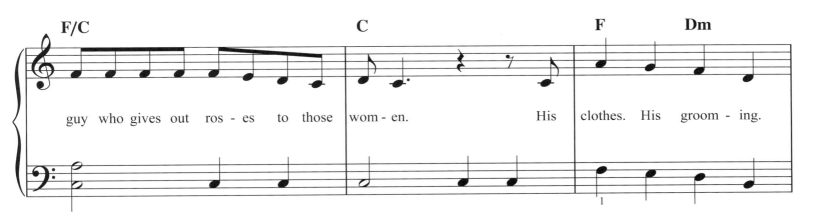

guy who gives out ros - es to those wom - en. His clothes. His groom - ing.

And he's a foot a-way from me; with swoop-y hair and shin-y eyes that I could swim in. He is

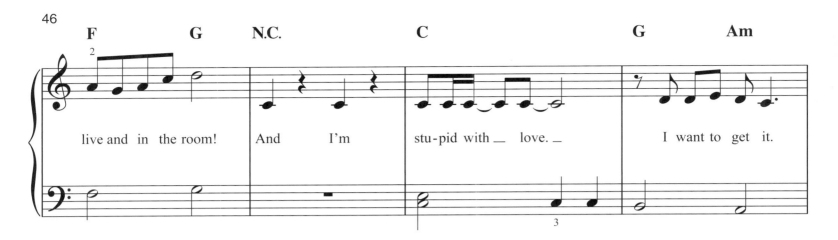

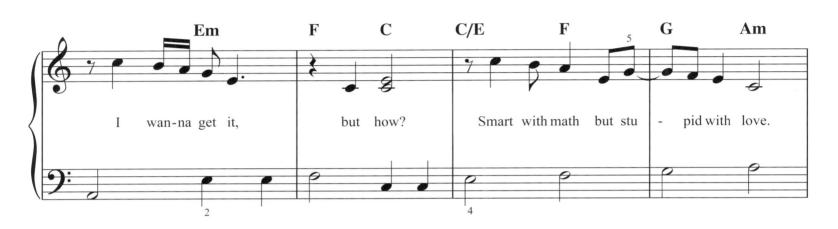

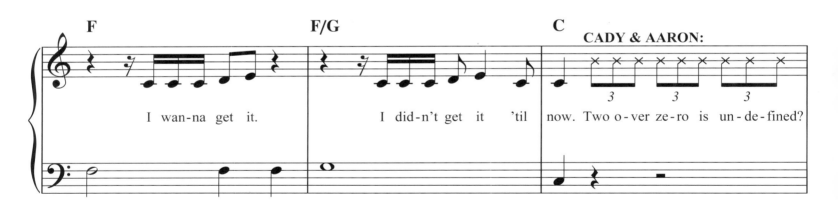

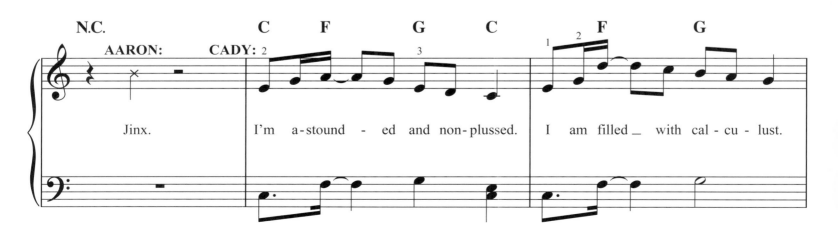

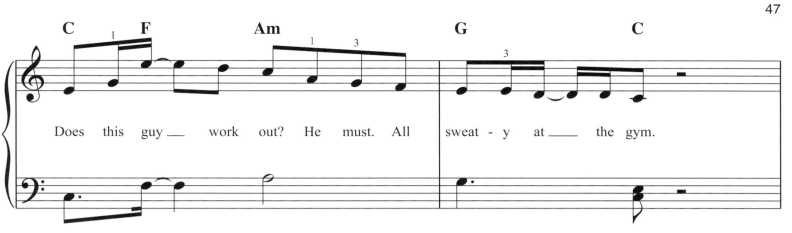

Does this guy __ work out? He must. All sweat-y at __ the gym.

Could that im - age be more hot? Let me just __ en - joy that thought.

School was rough, __ but now? It's not! 'Cause now there's him.

It's all so sim - ple! Stu-pid with __ love. __ But I can get it.

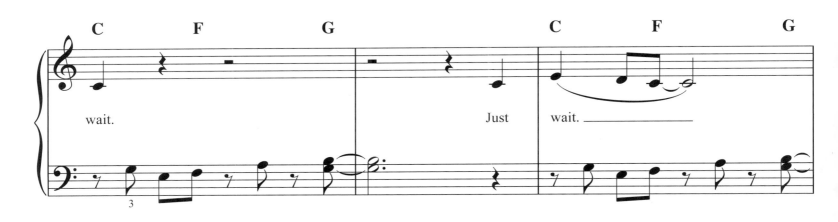

WHERE DO YOU BELONG?

Words by NELL BENJAMIN
Music by JEFF RICHMOND

Copyright © 2018 Useful Yak Music and Jeffrey Richmond Music
All Rights Administered Worldwide by Kobalt Songs Music Publishing
All Rights Reserved   Used by Permission

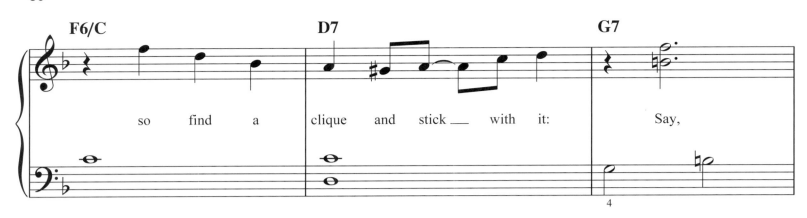

F6/C   **D7**   **G7**

so find a clique and stick __ with it: Say,

C9sus   **F**   **C**

where __ do you be - long? *Let's take a walk* *around the cafeteria, shall we?*

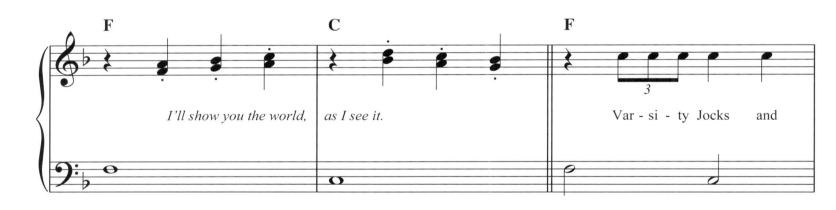

F   **C**   **F**

I'll show you the world, *as I see it.* Var - si - ty Jocks and

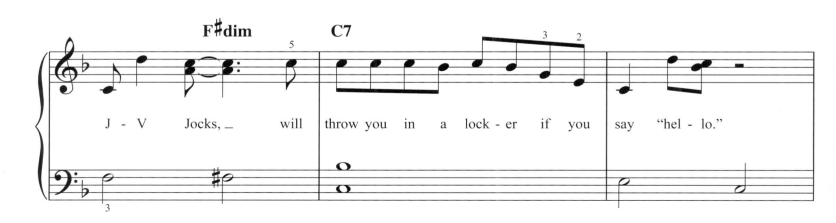

F#dim   **C7**

J - V Jocks, __ will throw you in a lock - er if you say "hel - lo."

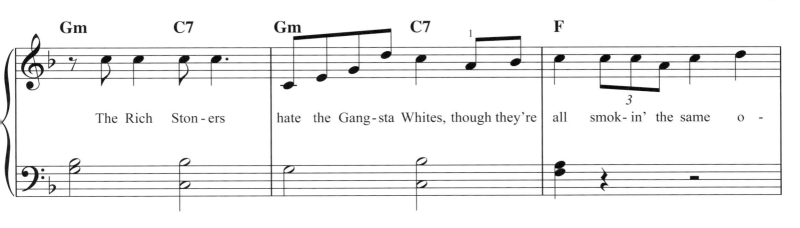

The Rich Ston-ers hate the Gang-sta Whites, though they're all smok-in' the same o-

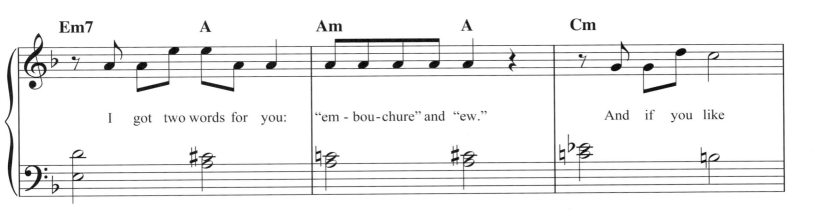

reg - a - no. ____ Here's the Sex-'lly Ac-tive Band Geeks.

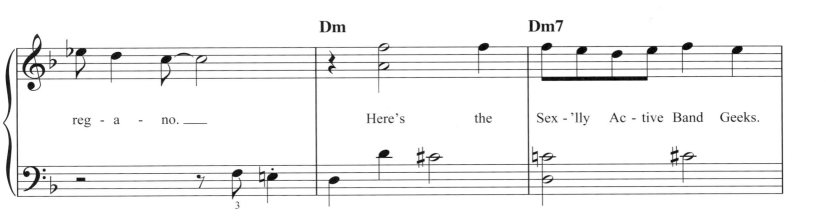

I got two words for you: "em - bou - chure" and "ew." And if you like

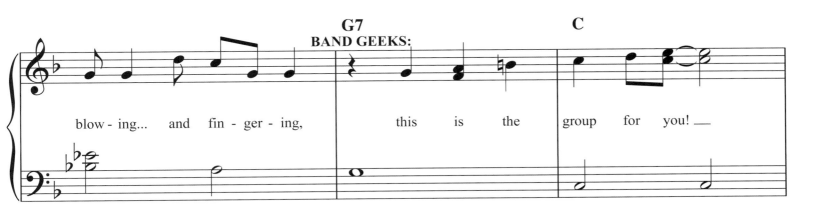

BAND GEEKS:

blow - ing... and fin - ger - ing, this is the group for you! ____

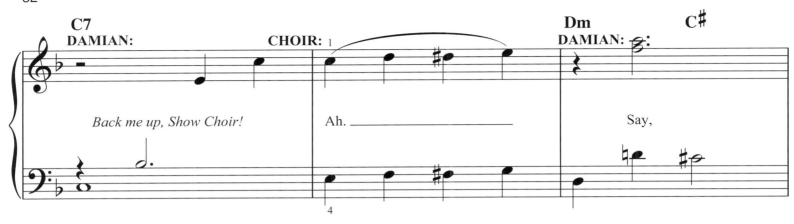

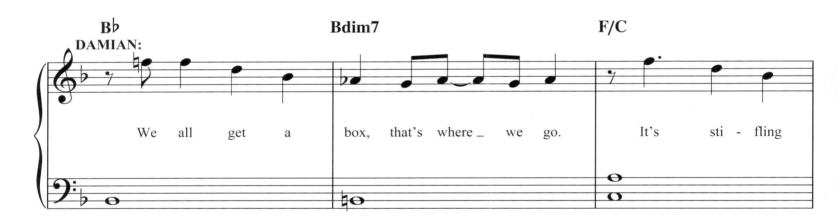

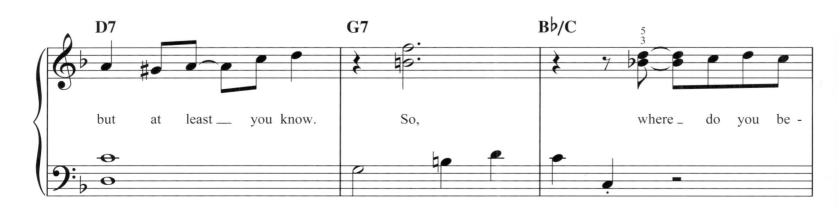

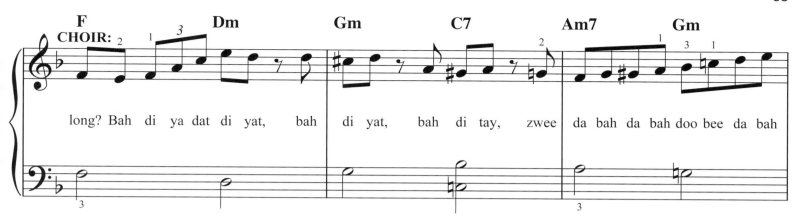

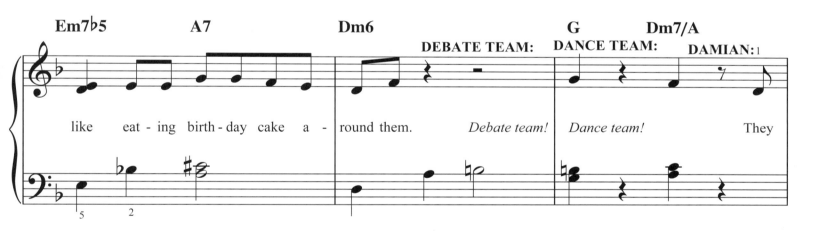

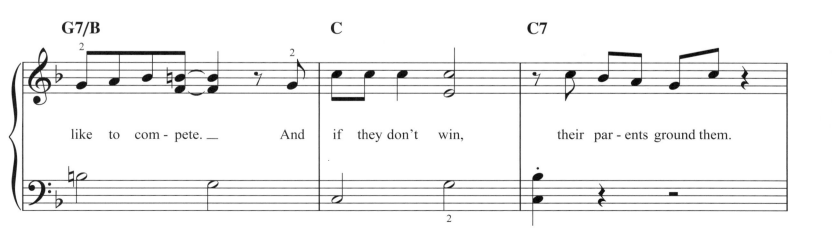

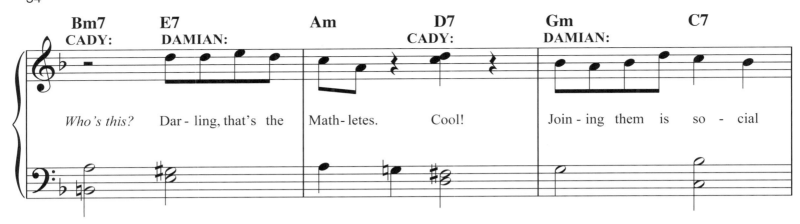

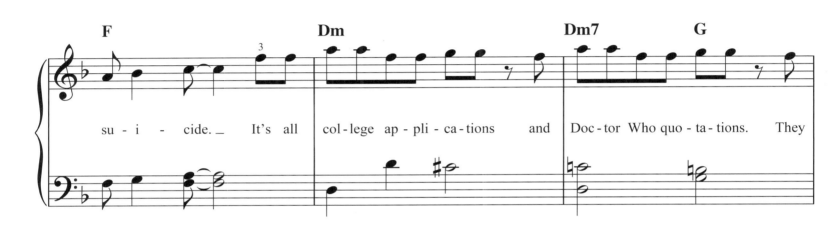

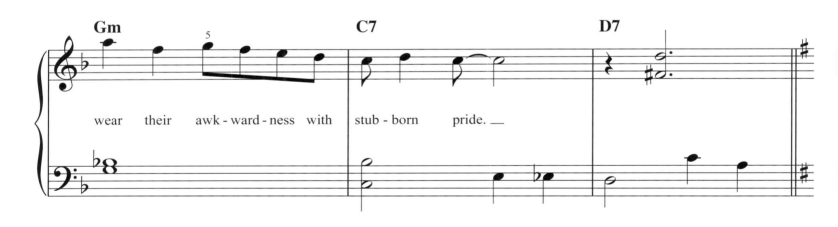

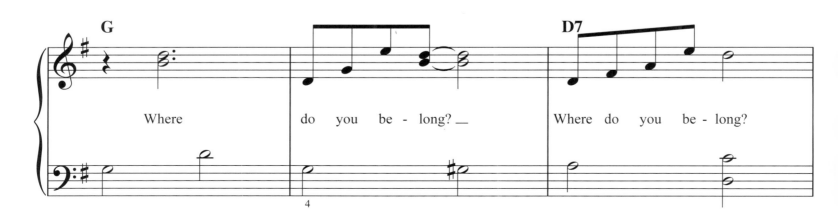

Where do you be - long? __

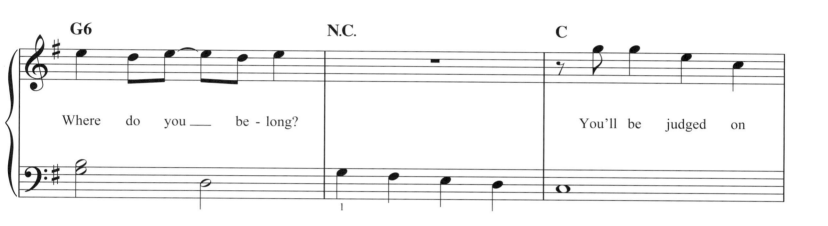

Where do you __ be - long?   You'll be judged on

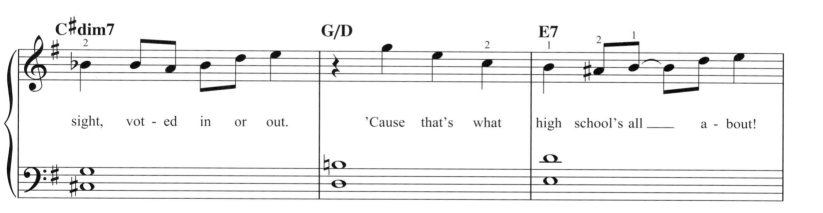

sight, vot - ed in or out. 'Cause that's what high school's all __ a - bout!

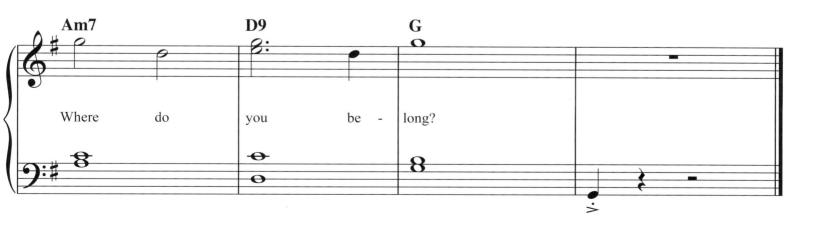

Where do you be - long?

WHAT'S WRONG WITH ME?

Words by NELL BENJAMIN
Music by JEFF RICHMOND

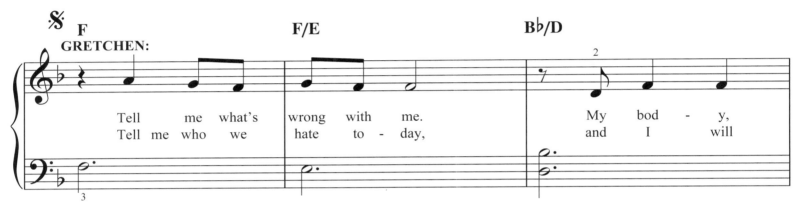

Copyright © 2018 Useful Yak Music and Jeffrey Richmond Music
All Rights Administered Worldwide by Kobalt Songs Music Publishing
All Rights Reserved   Used by Permission

and we both know you're right. __ I could lis - ten to you, __
there'll be blood on the floor. __ But which one will be - tray __

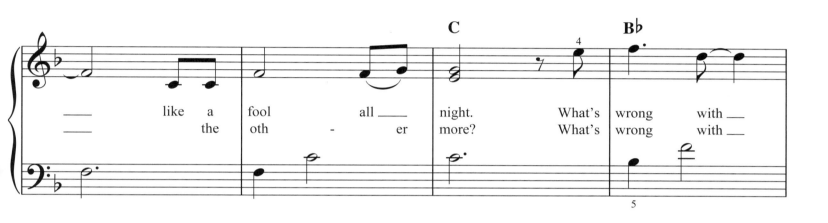

like a fool all __ night. What's wrong with __
the oth - er more? What's wrong with __

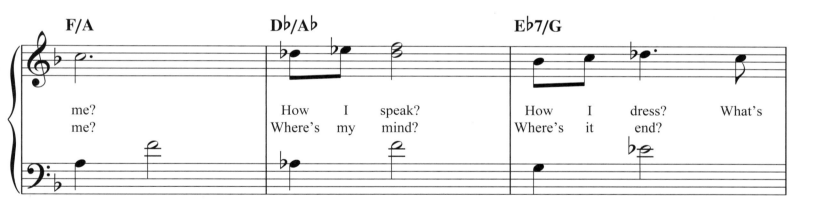

me? How I speak? What's
me? Where's my mind? How I dress? What's
Where's it end?

To Coda ⊕

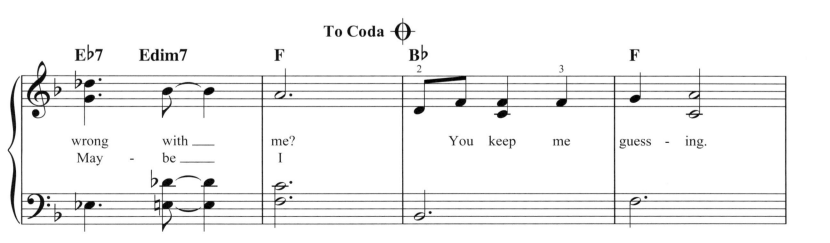

wrong with __ me? You keep me guess - ing.
May - be __ I

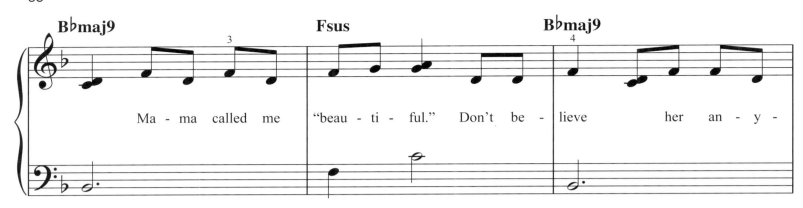

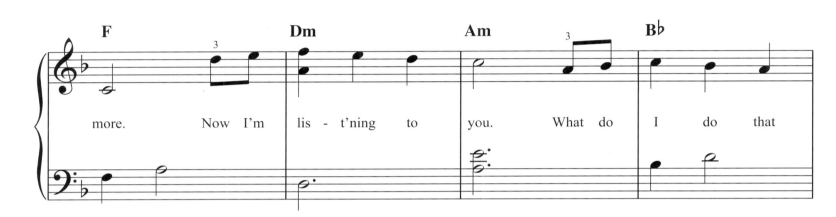

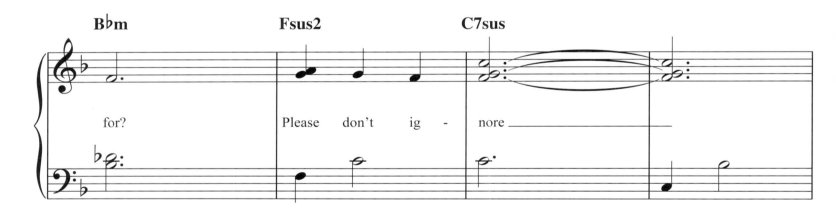

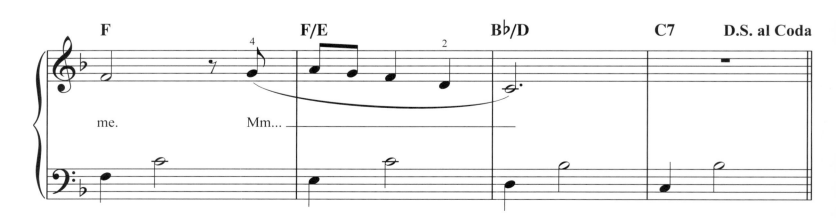

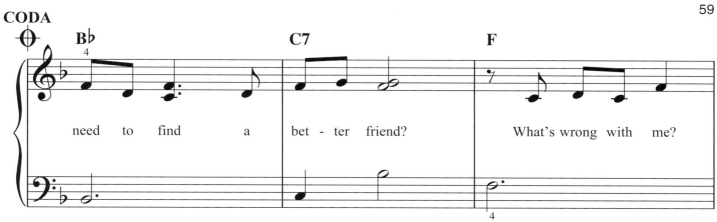

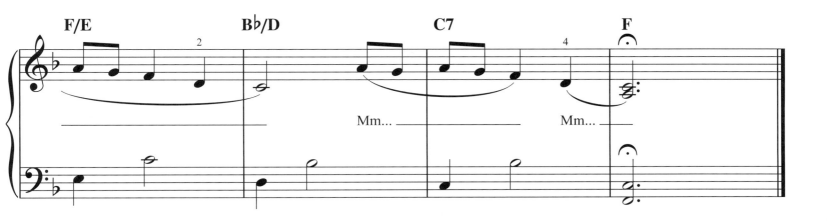

WORLD BURN

Words by NELL BENJAMIN
Music by JEFF RICHMOND

Stormy

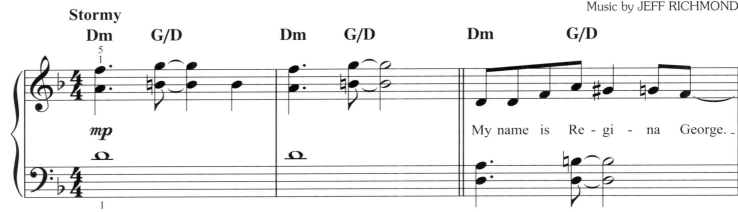

My name is Re - gi - na George.

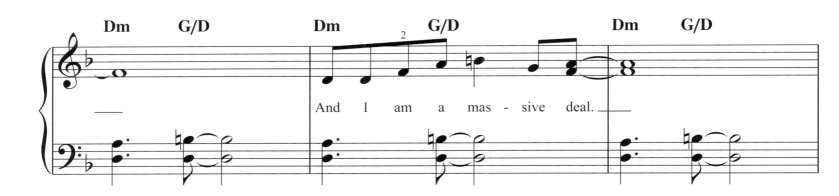

And I am a mas - sive deal.

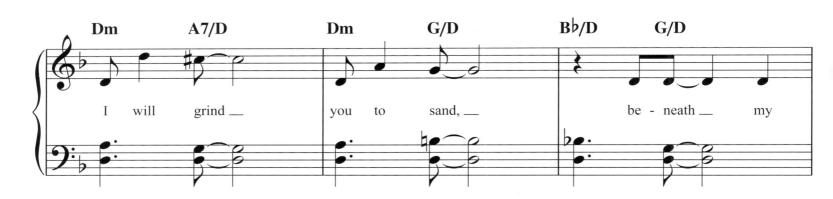

I will grind ___ you to sand, ___ be - neath ___ my

Lou - bou - tined heel. This is what ___ I get for help - ing,

Copyright © 2018 Useful Yak Music and Jeffrey Richmond Music
All Rights Administered Worldwide by Kobalt Songs Music Publishing
All Rights Reserved   Used by Permission

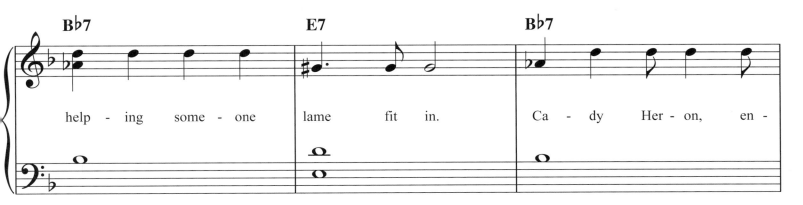

help - ing some - one lame fit in. Ca - dy Her - on, en -

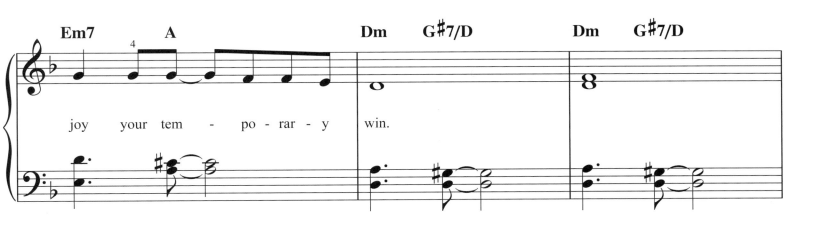

joy your tem - po - rar - y win.

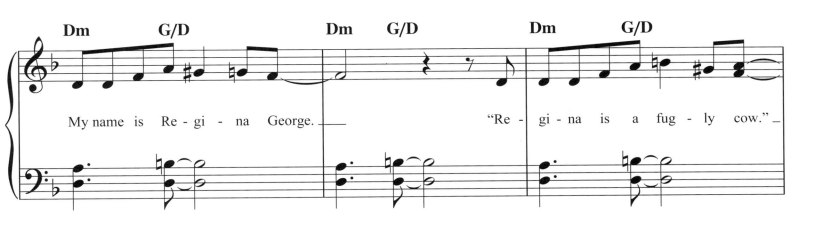

My name is Re - gi - na George. ___ "Re - gi - na is a fug - ly cow." ___

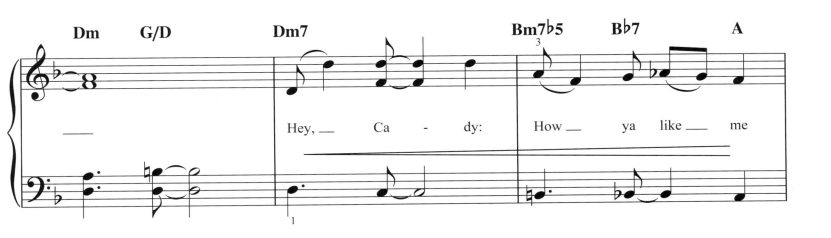

___ Hey, ___ Ca - dy: How ___ ya like ___ me

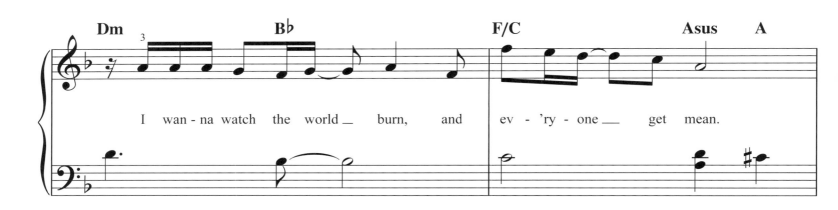

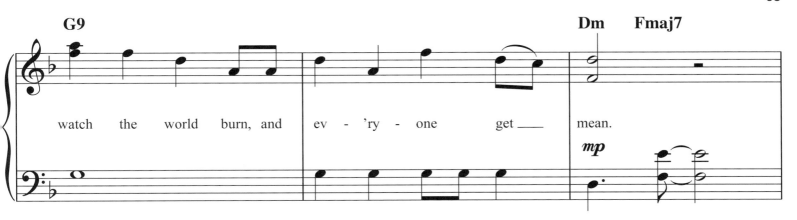

watch the world burn, and ev - 'ry - one get ___ mean.

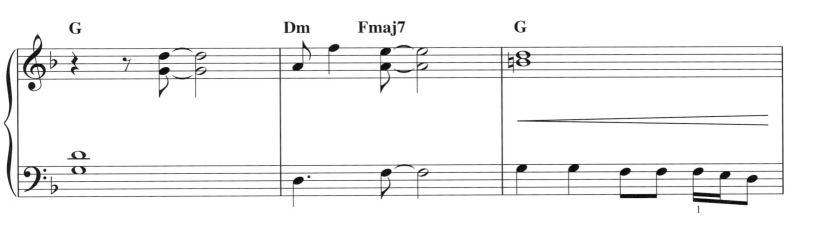

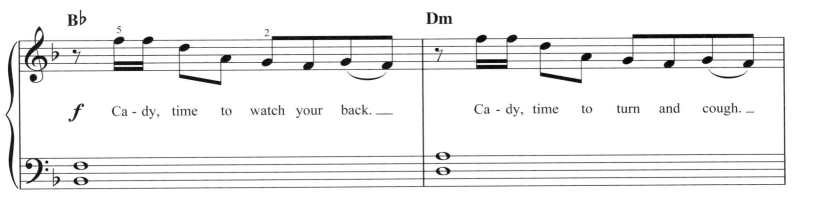

Ca - dy, time to watch your back. ___ Ca - dy, time to turn and cough. ___

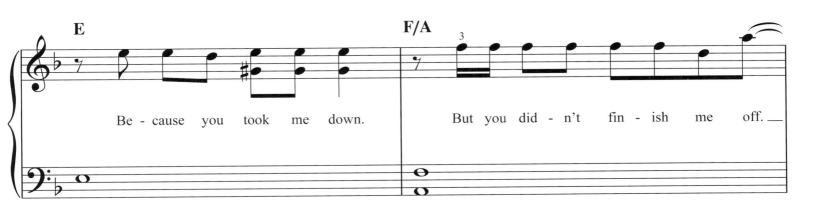

Be - cause you took me down. But you did - n't fin - ish me off. ___

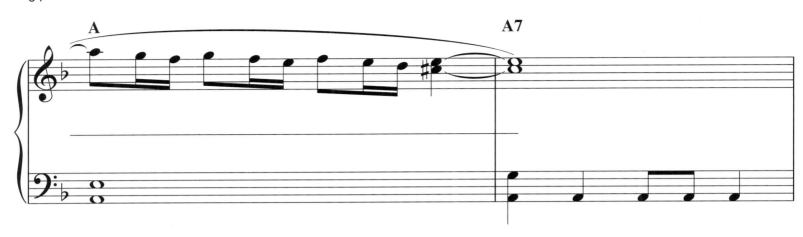

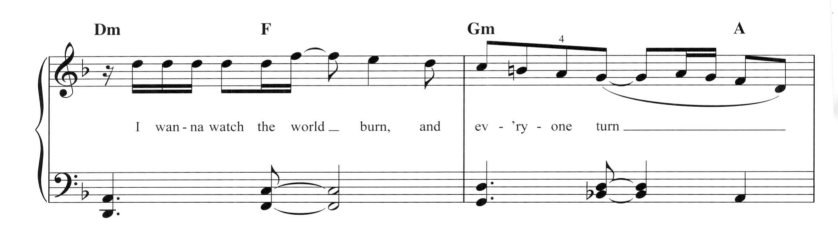

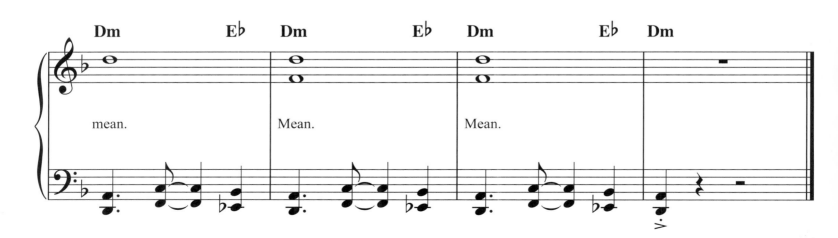